G000124145

Sex Before Marriage

Marriage

....

How Far Is Too Far?

Timothy S. Lane

New
Growth
Press

www.newgrowthpress.com

New Growth Press, Greensboro, NC 27404
Copyright © 2009 by Christian Counseling & Educational Foundation. All rights reserved. Published 2009.

Typesetting: Robin Black, www.blackbirdcreative.biz

ISBN-10: 1-935273-17-5
ISBN-13: 978-1-935273-17-2

Library of Congress Cataloging-in-Publication Data

Lane, Timothy S.
  Sex before marriage : how far is too far? / Timothy S. Lane.
     p. cm.
  Includes bibliographical references and index.
  ISBN-13: 978-1-935273-17-2 (alk. paper)
  ISBN-10: 1-935273-17-5 (alk. paper)
  1. Sex—Religious aspects—Christianity. 2. Marriage—
Religious aspects—Christianity. I. Title.
  BT708.L427 2009
  241'.66—dc22

                              2009031689

Printed in Canada

21 20 19 18 17 16 15 14   7 8 9 10 11

"We love each other and are faithful to each other, so I don't think there's anything wrong with having sex before we get married."

"Isn't it a good idea to see if we're sexually compatible before we get married?"

"Don't make sex before marriage into such a big deal—everyone does it."

"I'm not going to let other people make me feel guilty just because I don't buy into their value system."

Have you ever thought or said things like this? If your answer is yes, you have a lot of company. Most people, at least in some circumstances, think premarital sex is okay. What was once frowned upon is now an accepted part of Western culture, and sex education usually means learning about "safe sex," and how to take steps to avoid unwanted pregnancy and sexually transmitted diseases. But you have probably noticed that education about "safe sex" hasn't protected those around you from experiencing hurt and broken relationships as they have experimented sexually. Since God made you and also created sex, why not take the time to look at what he has to say about your sexuality and how it should be expressed? You may be surprised at what you learn.

Christians haven't always done a very good job talking about sex. Some avoid the topic all together, and others give the impression that sex is somehow inherently degrading and tainted. But God, in the Bible, doesn't avoid the topic of sex or say that it is bad. Instead, God has a positive view of sex and also specific guidelines about how to express your sexuality. God is not a killjoy—his guidelines for your sexuality are for your help, protection, and good.

What God Thinks About Sex

While the church has not always addressed the issue of sex in helpful ways, the Bible does. The most realistic, hopeful, and wise handling of sex is found there. You can always count on the Bible's realism and directness. Biblical writers never shy away from controversial topics. They teach that the physical world is good and give guidance on how to rightfully enjoy it. This is true of sex as well.

Many people think that God, in the Bible, says that sex is inherently bad and sinful, but nothing could be further from the truth. At the very beginning, God looked at everything he created and said it was "very good" (Genesis 1:31). Even after sin entered into the world, the Bible never speaks of the physical world as inherently sinful. People do use physical things in wrong ways, but that doesn't make physical activities like eating or sex wrong.

If you have any doubts that sex is part of the goodness of God's creation, look at the Song of Solomon, a small book in the Old Testament section of the Bible. It's a series of joyful poems written by a bride and a groom about the physical expression of love in marriage. When you read this, you will know that the Bible is not squeamish about sex. Here's one of many passages that celebrates marital sexual intimacy:

The bridegroom begins by saying,

"You have stolen my heart, my sister, my bride; you have stolen my heart with one glance of your eyes, with one jewel of your necklace.

How delightful is your love, my sister, my bride! How much more pleasing is your love than wine, and the fragrance of your perfume than any spice! Your lips drop sweetness as the honeycomb, my bride; milk and honey are under your tongue. The fragrance of your garments is like that of Lebanon. You are a garden locked up, my sister, my bride; you are a spring enclosed, a sealed fountain." (Song of Solomon 4:9–12)

And his bride responds,

"My lover has gone down to his garden, to the beds of spices, to browse in the gardens and to gather lilies. I am my lover's and my lover is mine; he browses among the lilies." (Song of Solomon 6:2–3)

These love poems brim with a positive view of sex in marriage. In the New Testament, the apostle Paul also affirms the goodness of the physical world. Paul says that your body "is not meant for sexual immorality, but for the Lord, and the Lord for the body. And God raised the Lord and will also raise us up by his power. Do you not know that your bodies are members of Christ?" (1 Corinthians 6:13–15, ESV). Paul is reminding us that Jesus' physical body was raised from the dead, so all those who believe in him will also be raised from the dead. Our physical bodies are one with Christ himself! This is a resounding affirmation of physical bodies. Paul goes on to say that our bodies are temples of the Holy Spirit (1 Corinthians 6:19). Because the body is good, sex and other physical activities can be enjoyed to the glory of God with no sense of shame. God intends married couples to celebrate and enjoy sex.

Sex Is Not a Casual Activity

Paul also says that our bodies were not meant for sexual immorality (1 Corinthians 6:13). The word Paul uses for sexual immorality is the Greek word "porneia." This is a very comprehensive word used in the Bible to describe any and all kinds of sexual behavior outside the context of marriage between a man and a woman. Paul takes sexual sin very seriously and includes it in a long list of sins (both sexual and nonsexual) that have temporal and eternal consequences (1 Corinthians 6:9). His attitude towards sexual sin comes from God. God places a high value on sex—after all he invented it (Genesis 1:28; 2:18–25)! He also bases it upon the teachings of Jesus in Matthew 5:27–30 and 19:4–6. The Bible celebrates sex within marriage, but never talks about it as something that is casual because it is not a casual activity.

The Right Way to Enjoy Sex

Paul says that sex is good, but there is a proper context for enjoying our sexuality. Sex is rightfully enjoyed within the context of an exclusive, heterosexual marriage. Paul does not say it's okay to have sex if you really, really like one another and plan to be in a highly committed dating relationship. No, Paul says that intimate sexual relations should be reserved exclusively for two people who have entered into a commitment with one another in a religious or civil ceremony. A marriage is created when a man and a woman go on record in a public and legal context to acknowledge their commitment to one another.

What makes a marriage is a covenant or legal commitment, so until you make that commitment with someone, you aren't married. Certainly marriage is much more than the beginning commitment or promise, but it is never less than that.

Why does it seem like the Bible is so narrow in how you practice and enjoy sex? The answer is that God knows how powerful sex is. When sex is practiced outside of marriage, you are misusing it and there are personal and interpersonal consequences. Sex outside of marriage is incomplete, because it doesn't have a binding union as its basis. So when you have sex outside of marriage, what you are really saying is, "I want to have physical union with you, but not the entanglements of any other kind of binding union." Most people don't consciously think like that when they are having sex before marriage, yet, that is what they are doing and communicating—no matter how much they say they care for their partner.

Married sex is very powerful. It communicates the intense, personal nature of the marriage bond. The Hebrew word for sex is *yada,* which literally means to know someone personally. Sex is a form of disclosing yourself to another—becoming vulnerable and open in a very personal way that leads to an intimate knowledge of another. Every time a husband and wife have sex, it is a way of recommitting themselves to one another. They are saying that they belong exclusively to one another and no one else. To have sex in a casual way goes against the grain of what sex was intended to communicate. It was never intended to be a casual, recreational activity that can be done with someone outside of the context of deep commitment and love. When you use sex like this, even though it might feel great, in the long run there is bound to be hurt and pain.

Maybe the metaphor of fire will help you to understand the difference between premarital sex and sex in marriage. If you make a fire and keep it in the fireplace, it brings warmth and comfort to those around it. But if you take that same fire out of the fireplace, it will destroy the whole house and harm those who live there. So it is with sex and marriage. This is how C. S. Lewis puts it in *Mere Christianity:*

The Christian idea of marriage is based on Christ's words that a man and wife are to be regarded as a single organism....The male and female were made to be combined together in pairs, not simply on a sexual level, but totally combined. The monstrosity of sexual intercourse outside of marriage is that those who indulge in it are trying to isolate one kind of union (the sexual) from all the other kinds of union which were intended to go along with it and make up the total union. The Christian attitude does not mean that there is anything wrong about sexual pleasure, any more than about the pleasure of eating. It means that you must not isolate that pleasure and try to get it by itself, any more than you ought to try to get the pleasures of taste without swallowing and digesting, by chewing things and spitting them out again.[1]

Often people reject Christian values because they don't understand why these values have been given. They think that God is too strict and is trying to keep them from enjoying life. But God doesn't want to keep you from enjoying his world; he wants you to enjoy it more! So he has put guardrails around your sexuality to keep it within marriage. The Song of Solomon repeats this phrase three times: "Promise me...not to awaken love until the time is right" (Song of Solomon 2:7; 3:5; 8:4, NLT). The right time for love to be awakened and ultimately fulfilled is when you are married.

Doesn't it make sense that the one who made you and your sexuality would also know how it should be used? His guidelines are given to help you enjoy your sexuality and to protect you from harming yourself and others. Sex is a wonderful gift from God, and he wants you to enjoy it and all of his good gifts in ways that are good and true.

Some Common Objections to "Waiting"

It's no secret that sex is a pleasurable activity—whether you are married or not. When something *feels* good, it is easy to think up reasons for why it *is* good. Here are two common objections I've heard in my counseling for why we shouldn't wait until marriage for sex and intimacy.

1. Lots of married couples have horrible sex and unmarried couples have great sex. Can something that feels so good really be wrong? And, isn't it better to practice?

While it might be true that some married couples don't have a good sexual relationship and some unmarried couples do, you shouldn't decide whether something is right or wrong based on anecdotes. That's a very subjective approach to deciding your values. Sadly, I have counseled many people who regret having sexual intimacy outside of marriage. I've also talked with countless married couples, of all different ages, who have a vibrant sexual relationship. Still, these are just more anecdotes. When making decisions, instead of using anecdotes, we need to base our decisions on a standard outside of ourselves. The Bible tells us that there is a wise, loving, gracious, and personal God who made us and knows what is best for us. His commands are not capricious; they are for our good. He is not trying to spoil our fun. Instead, he wants us to learn how to delight in his world and in our sexuality in the context of marriage. Having sex outside of marriage is not "good practice." Sex is not a matter of learning skills; it is about learning to sacrificially love someone in the context of an exclusive marital relationship.

2. Isn't it true that desiring sex and food is the same thing since both are physiological needs? If you don't eat, it is not good for you. So isn't it also true that if you deny yourself sex, it is not good for you either?

Interestingly enough, the Corinthians had a similar line of argument that Paul addresses in 1 Corinthians 6:12–13:

> "Everything is permissible for me"—but not everything is beneficial. "Everything is permissible for me"—but I will not be mastered by anything. "Food for the stomach and the stomach for food"—but God will destroy them both. The body is not meant for sexual immorality, but for the Lord, and the Lord for the body.

Notice how Paul qualifies his emphasis on Christian liberty. He says that everything is permissible that is not obviously sinful. But he adds two qualifications:

Is it beneficial? And will it become enslaving? Then he addresses the whole issue of eating and sex and shows how they are not the same. Paul says that there is a difference between food that is eaten, digested, and passed through the body and sexual intercourse. Sex cannot be dismissed as a purely physiological activity, because it affects the whole body and soul of the two people who engage in sex. And finally, here is the most obvious point: if you don't eat you will eventually die, but if you don't have sex you will not die. Feeding the fire of sexual desire has never calmed the temptation; it only increases the desire.

How Far Is Too Far?

Perhaps you already agree that you shouldn't have sex before marriage, and for you the most pressing question is, "How far can I go as a single adult and still be sexually pure?" While this question might be motivated by seeing how much you can get away with in a relationship, it can also be a good, honest question about how to maintain sexual purity in a world with few boundaries. In biblical times and even well into the twentieth century, marriages were arranged not by individuals, but by families. People tended to marry at a much younger age, often in their early teens. Today most Western cultures have moved in the direction of "dating," with individuals meeting and finding their own spouse without family input, and more people are waiting to get married until their mid to late twenties. So young people are remaining single for a much longer period of time, have fewer restrictions on sexual activity from society, and are thus more susceptible to the temptations of sexual involvement prior to marriage.

So what does it look like to be sexually pure in the twenty-first century? Here's an overarching principle to use as you try to answer that question: Don't act like you are married when you are not! When you are married, you make an exclusive commitment to one another. Within that context, you also commit to do everything possible to serve one another in every way including sexually. If you are not married, then you should avoid the physical activity that goes with a formal, exclusive commitment to one another.

But what does this mean in practice? How far is too far? Many Christians agonize over this question and struggle with guilt because they think they have crossed a line. Some single couples make vows to not hold hands or kiss until they are married. How does Scripture address this whole question? On one hand, the Bible does not give detailed regulations for how non-married people should relate because of the differences in historical context and practice that we just mentioned at the beginning of this section. On the other hand, the Bible is not silent. In light of the positive case the Bible makes for sex inside of marriage, and the warnings it gives to those who practice sex outside of marriage, we can conclude that any romantic and physical intimacy that is reserved for marriage should not be practiced outside of marriage. This means different things for different relationships.

Sexual Purity for Single Non-Dating Friends

Sexual purity for single non-dating friends means no romantic, physical contact at all. That means no "friend with benefits," "hooking up," "phone sex," or "sexting."

These phrases are common ways to describe friendships that include sexual involvement with a clear commitment to NO commitment by either person. Each person views the other as an informal outlet for sexual "needs." Any of these practices would be a violation of God's wise and loving commands to keep any and all sexual contact and conduct within marriage. Remember that sex is powerful. It is not a casual activity and when you treat it like it is, it is hurtful to yourself and others. None of these practices express a true friendship where you put aside your own desires and do what is best for someone else. Instead of using each other for mutual satisfaction, friends are called to lay down their lives for one another.

Sexual Purity for Singles Who Are Dating

Since modern dating was not the habit when the Bible was written, answering this question requires careful reflection and the application of general guidelines of biblical wisdom. Scripture is always asking, "What does it look like to love and serve the other person in such a way that they are encouraged to grow in grace?" This should be the fundamental starting point for all of your decisions involving physical contact with someone you are dating.

Practically this means not doing anything that may hinder your date's growth in grace or create problems for him or her now and in the future. Can a couple hold hands? Is it permissible to kiss? These seem to be questions where there is a strong measure of freedom. Factors that impact how you apply the Bible to this situation are shaped in some measure by the situation. A couple in their early teens, a couple that just started dating, and a couple that is thinking about marriage might each draw boundaries in different places.

How can you tell if even holding hands and kissing is going too far? Whenever your romantic activity leads to more involved physical touching, that seemingly harmless physical involvement should be up for discussion. If you, as a couple, are moving in the direction of doing things that are reserved for marriage, then questions should be asked. Deep, exclusive romantic involvement should not be the norm in a person's life unless the relationship is moving towards marriage. Touching that leads to undue stimulation that can only be satisfied by an orgasm or sexual intercourse should be avoided.

If you are engaged, remember you are not married yet, so the same general principle of saving sex for marriage applies. If you can avoid it, don't plan an overly long engagement. Don't let the expectations of a perfect wedding with elaborate fanfare be the deciding factor for when you get married. Sometimes long engagements are necessary, but they can also increase temptation and put couples in a very difficult place as they seek to honor Christ.

What You Need to Do

If you have been pursuing sexual purity, then continue to rely upon God's help to remain pure. But if you have failed, and you are reading this and reflecting on God's perspective on your sexuality, you may think that there's no hope for you. You see how far you have fallen short of God's standard and how you have misused sex. But God has a message of hope for you. In the same passage where Paul discusses sexual immorality he says this: "And that is what some of you were. But you were washed, you were sanctified, you were justified in the name of the Lord Jesus Christ and by the Spirit of our God" (1 Corinthians 6:11).

Paul was writing to a church in the ancient city of Corinth. The Corinthians' perspective on sexuality was very similar to ours. So, just like in our culture, sexual promiscuity was rampant. And because of that, brokenness was also rampant. Paul brought to them the message of God's forgiving grace in Christ. And look what was happening—they were being rescued, forgiven, and purified. Jesus, through his Spirit, had liberated them from a life of immorality and brokenness. That does not mean that there were no consequences to their actions, but it did mean that the past was forgiven and they were being given grace to change and grow in the present.

Find Grace and Forgiveness in Christ

If you are currently sexually active and not married, God's grace can give you the strength to grow and change, just as it did for the Corinthians. Freedom starts when you come to him and admit that you have misused your sexuality and by doing so have not loved others as you should. This is humbling, but remember, "God opposes the proud but gives grace to the humble" (James 4:6). There is grace and forgiveness for those who honestly tell God all about their failures and sins and ask for help. Jesus came to this earth, lived the perfect life you are not able to live, and died in your place to pay for all of your sins. Put your hope in him and you will never be disappointed. He will give you the desire to change your sexual behavior and his Spirit will lead you, step by small step, to make the necessary changes in your relationships with others. And when you fail, as we all do, simply go back to the beginning—ask for forgiveness and help. Grace is for the humble, not the perfect.

Start Talking

Now extend your honest conversation to include the person with whom you are in a relationship. Perhaps this is a topic you haven't really talked about—you've assumed you know what the other person is thinking or feeling. So begin talking candidly about your relationship, including your sexual involvement. Don't let the fear of losing the relationship keep you from doing this. You might feel like God is asking you to give up something you can't live without. But Jesus' words are true; we must die to our self-centered desires if we are ever going to really live (Matthew 10:38–39). This is the irony of God's grace. At just the moment when we feel like we are dying to something we think we must have to be happy, he gives us so much more than we ever imagined. As C.S. Lewis says,

> Our Lord finds our desires, not too strong,
> but too weak. We are half-hearted creatures,
> fooling about with drink and sex and ambition
> when infinite joy is offered us, like an ignorant
> child who wants to go on making mud pies in a
> slum because he cannot imagine what is meant
> by the offer of a holiday at the sea. We are far
> too easily pleased.[2]

Don't avoid talking with your partner because you don't want to lose the momentary pleasure of sex. This will be very tempting, but following Christ sometimes means giving up things you desire because you love him and trust that he knows what's best for you. Pray for God to give you strength and resolve to pursue the kind of lifestyle that will please him and benefit others.

Fight Temptation

Your willpower alone will not help you in this fight, especially if you are already sexually active with someone. You need to actively fight against the temptation to use your sexuality in ways that are not truly loving. Temptation, even to physical sins, starts with what you desire and want more than your relationship with God (James 1:14–15). So look at what is going on inside of you. What do you desire that is fueling your sexual behavior? Pleasure? Excitement? Power? Companionship? Attention? Identity? Only you can answer this question. Take the time to think this through and, if you are in a long-term relationship, talk it through with your partner. Understanding your motivation will help you to honestly confess to God and your partner where you are wrong. It might mean that you should consider pursuing marriage. But just because you are having sex does not make you married or mean that you should get married. You are married only when you enter into a public, legal commitment with each other.

If you are serious about giving up your unwise behavior, you should think through, again with your partner, how and where you spend time together. As you do this, ask God for help. Remember, "No temptation has seized you except what is common to man. And God is faithful; he will not let you be tempted beyond what you can bear. But when you are tempted, he will also provide a way out so that you can stand up under it" (1 Corinthians 10:13). The phrase "way out" is taken from the idea of journeying through a mountain path with discipline and care. So the way of escape from temptation that God promises doesn't mean a quick, easy solution, but instead a pathway out of a difficult place. For the Christian, the promise of Jesus' presence with you should be of great encouragement, comfort, and hope.

Be Accountable

One way to escape this temptation is to share your struggles in this area with a mature Christian friend, pastor, or counselor. Although all sin is hard to fight on your own, temptations that involve your body are particularly difficult to fight without the help of your fellow Christians. You need help from others who can guide you and walk with you through the decisions you need to make to grow in your commitment to a sexually pure life. Make sure the people you talk with understand God's perspective on sex, will pray with and for you in this area of struggle, and will remind you constantly that God's grace is for sinners, including those who have committed sexual sin.

Don't be discouraged if you fall back into sexual sin. Jesus died for your sins, and he stands ready to forgive you when you come to him in honest confession (1 John 1:9). And Jesus not only died for you, he also rose from the dead. His resurrection means that God's power is now available to all who call upon his name. It's his power that will change your deepest desires, so you will want your life—even your sex life—to please him in every way.

Whatever your sexual behavior is doing for you, it's nothing compared to the surpassing greatness of knowing Christ and becoming like him (Philippians 3:8).

Ask him every day for his Spirit to work in your life and change you to make you like him. Jesus knows all about your struggles and temptations, and he will help you find the "way of escape" through them. As he does so, you will have the opportunity to bring honor to him, to experience the blessing of living for him in our broken world, and to be a blessing in your relationships with the opposite sex.

Endnotes

1. C. S. Lewis, *Mere Christianity* (New York: Macmillan Publishing Co., 1952), 95-96.
2. C. S. Lewis, *The Weight of Glory and Other Addresses* (New York: Macmillan Publishing Co., 1980), 3-4.

Simple, Quick, Biblical

Advice on Complicated Counseling Issues for Pastors, Counselors, and Individuals

MINIBOOK
CATEGORIES

- Personal Change
- Marriage & Parenting
- Medical & Psychiatric Issues

- Women's Issues
- Singles
- Military

SE YOURSELF | GIVE TO A FRIEND | DISPLAY IN YOUR CHURCH OR MINISTRY